IF YOU CAN ...

LIVE LIKE

RILEY

A "PAWBOOK" FOR POSITIVE LIVING

NELL MARTIN

If You Can ... Live Like Riley
A "pawbook" for Positive Living

Nell Martin

2nd Edition, published 2017
Green Parrot Press
www.GreenParrotPress.com

1st Edition, published 2013

ISBN: 978-1541326187

Illustrations by Marcy Chapman (MarcyChapman.com)
Cover design by Clint Chapman (GreenParrotPress.com)
Cover portrait of Riley by Ann Moran

Katie,

This book is for you. Looking back, the relationship I had with my grandmother was the most influential one in my life, and I feel one of my greatest losses has been living so far from you that we have not had enough time together. Even though distance and schedules have separated us, you have been a treasure in my life from the day you were born.

So, my precious Katie, I offer this part of me to you. Take what is useful to you from these stories and add to them your own.

Author's Note:

This book remained unfinished for many years. Now, at 80, I have taken the time to "redo it." Tati Ticciati came into my life at just the right time. Without her patient , gentle spirit this "redo" would never have happened.

My editor, Clint Chapman, and my illustrator, Marcy Chapman, have been invaluable help completing this undertaking.

And, all of "you" that I have had the opportunity to meet on my journey ... have been my teachers.

Thanks a million!

Contents

Prologue
If You Can ... Live the Life Riley

Life is composed of ever evolving changes — many unpredictable, some positive and welcome, others that appear adverse and undesirable. As those inevitable changes have continuously recreated my life, I have found an amazing thing. Life supplies you with the capacity to uncover abilities and strengths you did not know you had. Hidden powers lying within us all, just waiting to be unearthed, will sometimes be dug up by something as simple as the tiny paws of a new puppy!

Riley was that puppy for me. His tiny paws helped me discover ways to embrace life changes, live in the moment, seize the day and *Say "Yes" to life "Now!"*

It is easy to follow Riley's philosophy...

If You Can ...

Always find your way home
Love others like you want to be loved
Never have a bad day
Sniff out what's new and different
Never hold a grudge
Dig to China
Learn to ask for what you want
Learn from the school of hard knocks
Travel with the windows down
Look for the good in everyone
Live in the now

A joyous life awaits you, *if you can ...* adopt this simple affirmative approach to living.

CHAPTER ONE

If You Can ...
Find Your Way Home
(Know Yourself)

If You Can ...

Find Your Way Home

W hen Riley (our Wheaten Terrier) was three, my husband Bill and I moved from our home in Florida to Manhattan, New York, where Bill had accepted a temporary staff position at Marble Collegiate Church. The condominium we rented was in an ideal location, but unfortunately we were told that the building rules refused to allow pets. So sadly and hesitantly, we set out to find loving dog-sitters who would keep and care for Riley while we were away on what we thought would be a short-term adventure in the Big City. As it turned out, after Bill moved to a permanent position at Trinity Episcopal Church, we stayed for over seven years.

Almost immediately, I decided I loved New York. But I missed Riley so much and I wanted him to be with us and also see Manhattan. So, after several weeks of bribing the concierge with my homemade brownies and freshly baked bread, I was granted permission to bring him for a visit.

We flew back to Sarasota, bought Riley a ticket, and boarded a non-stop flight to LaGuardia. I was a nervous wreck. Would he be terror-stricken? Would the temperature in the baggage compartment be suitable? Would the two-and-a-half hour flight be on time? Trying to calm and assure me, Delta explained that they successfully flew twenty-five thousand animals every year.

I still wasn't sure. So to be on the safe side, I brought the pilots some of my homemade brownies and a picture of Riley, telling them I was putting my trust in them to have a smooth flight.

We landed on time at LaGuardia and I headed straight for the baggage claim. Riley's crate appeared. He emerged from his imprisonment unscathed and began his adventure in Manhattan. He stuck his head out of the limousine window, seeming perfectly at ease riding down the eight-lane highway. When we pulled up to his new home, he walked right through the revolving glass doors, followed us into the elevator, up to the twenty-seventh floor, and pranced into his new abode. After sniffing out the place, he jumped up on the bed and took a nap, as if to say, "I need to rest a while."

At first, the sirens of New York, the horns blowing, and the absence of grass must have been very disconcerting to him. It was some time before he finally became comfortable doing his "business" on the sidewalk.

Surprisingly to me, New York turned out to be a very dog-friendly city. Outdoor restaurants welcomed Riley, as did Saks and Bloomingdales. He was a natural with escalators and even rode through Linens and Things in a pushcart. We found another Wheaten Terrier in our apartment building. Every day, Riley and his new found friend, Buster, romped around the penthouse terrace where Buster lived.

About a week after Riley arrived, Bill was walking him home from Woolworth's on 23rd Street, when a huge garbage truck hit a pothole. The loud crash startled Riley. He backed out of his collar and leash, tucked his tail between his legs, and took off running as fast as he could down the sidewalks of New York. Bill whistled, called, and ran after him, but to no avail. Riley got to the comer of 23rd and Broadway and was out of sight. Bill continued to search and call — No Riley. Finally he gave up and came back to the apartment to tell me the sad news of Riley's unfortunate disappearance. We were very upset!

A while later Tim, the concierge from the lobby, called. He said he'd just seen Riley come through the revolving doors of our apartment building and run to the elevator as though waiting for us. He was safe. No matter how scared Riley may have been, he sure knew how to find his way home.

I have often heard, "Home is where the heart is," a place of safety, where you can relax, feed your soul, and refresh yourself. On my journey through life, occasionally I have strayed, mentally and emotionally, far from that "home" place. Before I knew it, I got lost in a forest of chaos without a clear path back "home." There is an old saying, "When in danger, when in doubt, run in circles, scream and shout." Too many times in my life, that's exactly what I did. Usually, at some point, I would stop to catch my breath, and then realize — I'm lost.

Once in my life, I was lost for almost four years before I found my way back home. During the time we had moved to Manhattan, my mother and my father died, I finished graduate school, my husband retired, one of our children married, and my own marriage became strained. In the middle of all these circumstances, I was so busy reacting to everything that I simply forgot to take time to check-in with myself. I repressed my feelings and buried the pain of saying goodbye to so many things I loved.

Anti-depression medication helped and I was also seeing

a therapist, but before I recognized the severity of those tornadoes of change, the destruction had already become widespread. I put exercise on the back-burner and gained weight. I slept fitfully, waking up in the middle of the night anxious and tired. By that time, my therapist suggested I check into a treatment hospital for my depression. Trusting her judgment, I flew to Tucson, Arizona, and walked through the doors of the Sierra Tucson Treatment Hospital.

For four weeks, I cried through painting, drawing, exercising, and meditating while working my way back "home." I made new friends. Some were looking to reclaim their minds, some their hearts. Excellent therapists, well-trained in psychological map-making, were my companions as I rediscovered my way back to myself.

Today, I feel warm, safe, and at ease … at home. Knowing myself as I do, there's always a possibility it won't be the last time I become lost, "pull off my own leash," and have to find my way back. But maybe not!

I have discovered that life is much simpler than I've tried to make it. Observing Riley's uncomplicated approach to living has had a profound impact on the way I interact with the world around me. I believe I will always find my way "home" if I can … learn to love and be loved, accept the good in each day and each person, assertively seek what I want, live in the moment and enthusiastically say *"Yes"* to my ever-evolving existence.

 # CHAPTER TWO

If You Can …
Love Others Like
You Want To Be Loved

(Unconditional Love)

If You Can ...

Love Others Like You Want To Be Loved

My dog Riley loved us dearly and showed that love with his gift of "applause." Whether I was gone five minutes or five hours, his tail began to wag when he caught a glimpse or a scent of me. I've seen him get excited and ready to "applaud" as soon as he could hear my husband Bill's car approaching. We didn't have to do or give anything to get his approval — our very being was his joy to behold. His love was unconditional!

Isn't unconditional love what we all desire? To be valued because of who we are - not for what we do or don't do, not for what we have or don't have, or because we may or may not be gifted or beautiful. To walk onto the stage of life and receive "applause" with a standing ovation just because we "are" is ecstasy. That is a rare experience, if it ever happens. However, we do have the power to change that rarity. We could follow Riley's lead and, without condition, "applaud" others in the same way we want to be accepted and loved. Almost without fail, that "one-way" effort has the potential to evolve into a positive "two-way" experience.

Humans have a lot to learn about this kind of love. We are told, "God loves us unconditionally." I find this easy to believe, but hard to see, because I have rarely experienced it from another person. My grandmother Ethel came the closest. She delighted in me. Her eyes would shine as I entered the room. Not only did she warmly hold me, she always allowed me to hold her, to brush her hair, to play with her "Bo-Bo," (a name I gave to the mole on her stomach) and to feel her upper arm jiggle as I played with the softness of her aging body - which was so different from my lean, hard, small one.

I once heard Paul Tournier, the noted Swiss physician and author say, "All unsolicited suggestions are implied criticism." Grandmother very seldom made such promptings. She would give me five nickels and let me walk to town by myself and spend them any way I wanted. She never recommended that I might want to consider buying a paper-doll book with one of my nickels instead of another comic book.

When I would visit her, she would simply let me BE. I could swing with delight on an old rope swing hung on a branch or I could walk barefoot in the rain with Mr. Anderson, the postman, as he delivered mail up and down our block. Time was mine. When I wanted to talk, she would stop whatever she was doing, sit down on eye level with me and listen as though what I had to say was the most important thing in the world. She would tell me stories from the Bible and say over and over again, "God loves you as though you are his only child."

The most amazing thing was my grandmother was "no kin" to me. She was my step-grandmother. My blood grandmother had died about twenty years before I was born, and my grandfather, Thomas Lipscomb, a Methodist minister in Mississippi, married Ethel Golden. At the time, his youngest of five was eighteen months old and his oldest was nine.

Grandmother Ethel was an orphan and had been raised

by an aunt and uncle who were poor dirt farmers in rural Mississippi. Because of her intelligence, she received a scholarship and graduated from Mississippi State College for Women. Later she taught school at a Methodist orphanage, and that's where my granddaddy met her. We can find love in many places.

Like other children growing up in the Deep South, I also experienced some wonderful examples of love from members of the household help that were in our home. Some like Willie were more like my grandmother, having time for me, making very few "suggestions," and letting me be physically close. Willie lived in a one-room "house" in our backyard in Memphis. I loved the way it smelled on a cold day with the hint of kerosene she used to heat her home. Like my grandmother Ethel, her skin was soft, and if I felt lonely or scared, I could walk into Willie's space and feel safe.

As an adult, I guess "Mama Z" (Juanita Ziclos), was my "grandmother person." For forty years she was my "standing ovation." She delighted in me. I felt like she would stand in front of me to protect me from any and every fiery dragon.

Love is a word that is so "commonplace" that I think we seldom stop to examine, explain, or even feel it. Many books have been written about it. Romance novels sell by the million. We say, "I love that movie," "I love Christmas," or "I love my new car." What does that really mean? The longer I live, the more 1 realize how much I still have to learn about what love really is. Socrates once said, "Wisest is he who knows he doesn't know." So maybe I'm wise, even though not much of an expert about love.

When I was fourteen, I knew what love was — it was

the way I felt about Mickey. Would he call me tonight? Would he hold my hand during the movie? Practically all of my thoughts outside of the school hour (and sometimes during) were centered on Mickey. I thought I knew love, but in reality the longer I live the less I can explain, describe or understand it. What I know is I want to experience love in whatever place or form it happens to appear.

I believe that feeling is universal. Love is desired by everyone, yet the direct experience of it is as different for each person as the snowflakes that fall from the sky. We have distorted and distracted ideas about what love is, most fostered and reinforced by Madison Avenue imagery, fairy tales, romance novels, and popular songs. Love in our lives has become like Muzak in an elevator. We've become so accustomed to using the word "love," that we seldom take time to be aware of its presence, even when it surrounds us. Maybe our illusions about the different forms of love might cause us to miss it? One thing I do know, love is not static. The focus of it changes as we change and grow.

Years ago, I was shocked to hear someone say, "Hate is not the opposite of love, indifference is." That concept surprised me because I find myself indifferent to people, places, and things I once loved with all my heart. Psychological studies seem to help explain the "love we no longer feel," by saying those feelings were simply projections and that as we withdraw our projections, we can then learn to love. Learn to love? Has anyone ever learned to love? Love happens. It is a miracle that happens by grace. We cannot control it. We can be open to it, welcoming it when it happens, but we cannot make it happen.

We "ought" to love our parents, our children, our country,

and our God, but that's not always the case. At traditional celebrations like Thanksgiving and Christmas, love "ought" to be the focal point. Thinking of families I have observed, including my own, I have been saddened by the lack of love. This lack can be sensed even when families are gathered around a table full of beautiful crystal, china, and silver, laden with food trays that looked like they might have jumped off the pages of the newest Martha Stewart magazine. And, if you scratch beneath the surface, what might you find? Jealousy, unforgiving hurts, and competitiveness? Who is the pick of the litter? Why did "he" carve the turkey that way, not like Daddy did at all? Why can't she just relax like my mother did, instead of being so uptight about the rolls being too brown? Just think, a small quantity of Riley's unconditional acceptance would have the power to create such a different family picture. Even just a little "tail wagging" close to home might initiate a world changing domino effect.

Light has always overcome darkness, and we are promised that it always will. The universe is forever being reborn, and throughout the cycle of the new replacing the old, there is always abundance for all. Only when we become fearful do we fail to know this and take more than we need, hurting others. Love can be anywhere. It can be in the "Rileys," "Willies," "Mama Z's," grandmothers, and on and on. Ultimately it is our responsibility to find the love that fits our emptiness

I've read so many times "you can't love anyone else till you first love yourself." Yuck! That's not been my experience. Certainly, the more comfortable I am in my own skin, the less frightened I am; therefore the more available I am to love. There's one thing for sure, there's no shortage of love on our planet. The essence of God is love, and the spirit of God is everywhere. Maybe the problem, and the solution, is instead of making numerous demands about "how, who, where, and when" we can find love, we should "stop, look, and listen," and realize we're standing right in the middle of it! Accept it and share it — just like you would want to receive it.

CHAPTER THREE

If You Can ...
Never Have a Bad Day

(Acceptance, Balance, Contentment)

If You Can …

Never Have a Bad Day

Riley did not make judgments true or false, good or bad. Riley didn't have to "think about it," he simply lived his life in joyful hope. He would wake me every morning with a leap on the bed, giving me kisses, and then snuggling down beside me for his daily loving. After I scratched his ears and his tummy and told him what a good dog he was, he was ready to "carpe diem."

I believe Riley's practice of seizing the day, with a positive focus on the "what is," is the perfect recipe for never having a bad day. It is a way to recognize joy and happiness and a way to value their differences. Joy is being grateful for what I have. Joy is a knowing, while happy is a feeling. Happiness comes to me when I get something I want, something I think will fill a need in my heart. Of course, it does not last. It is tenuous and lacks depth. Joy, on the other hand, often comes uncalled-for and is the assurance that I live in a universe of abundance. Whenever I stop to appreciate the enormous creativity of God, I find joy is revealed to me. I do not need to chase after it. Joy, more profound than happiness, is a part of our creative energy. Joy is when we experience something beyond ourselves that feels safe, wonderful, awesome, and beautiful.

The sight of a baby often brings a touch of wonder to me. Seeing tiny fingers explore a ball of fluff on the blanket of the crib, watching the reaction to music from a toy strung across the playpen - that is truly joyful. I feel similar enthusiasm when I lose myself in a project of painting, or read with no schedule and the phone turned off or walk barefoot on the beach with gentle waves splashing my feet, or sit beside a mountain stream, touching the soft velvet green moss and marveling at the fragility of the bluets.

To stay close to the beauty of nature is to stay close to the heart of God. To contemplate with wonder the sound of the hummingbird, the beauty of an orchid, the softness of Riley's coat, and the gentleness in his eyes – these are ways to experience wonder, freedom, hope, and joy in life. When you do this, bad days are hard to find.

To me, hope feels softer, more accepting and less demanding than expectation. So I strive to abandon expectations and live with hope, choosing behavior that is good for me without making the results my main focus.

I remember one day going to my internist and during the examination being asked how I was. "Well, I'm not depressed, but I do feel hopeless. The world is in such a terrible spot. There are so many things that are going on that look like they're just going to get worse and worse."

When I left the office she gave me three prescriptions. When I handed the prescriptions to the pharmacist, she handed one back and said, "This is not a prescription for medicine. This is a prescription for hope." What the doctor had written was, "Quit watching television and reading the headlines. Do something kind for someone each day. Get involved in a community project that you know can make a difference."

That insightful doctor profoundly influenced the way I think about hope. Hope is more than optimism, it is a purpose. To live without a purpose is to shrivel up. When you observe what's going on around you and find a way to connect your life with the possibility of being part of a solution, you discover your plan and purpose. My purpose has always been the same, to love and there are many ways to accomplish that.

Repeatedly, we read about hope, trust and joy in the Bible. Nothing can separate me from the knowing of "All will be well." Although I cannot presume to define what "well" is, my job is to know, to trust, and to hope. My job is to recognize I am not only a human being on a spiritual journey, but also a spiritual being on a human journey.

I acknowledge that I am not the one in charge when I accept that God is the universal creator of my life's plan. However, I understand that He expects me to be a co-creator of my life as well. It is imperative to never let friends, family or the world around me write my script for me. If I do, I'll be left to wonder, where is my serenity? On no occasion does my happiness have to be dependent on others, "things," or external influences. As I grow older I better understand a plaque that hangs by my front door with the message, "The best things in life aren't things."

How do I accomplish this task of changing my thinking? One day at a time, I suppose. I need to remember to breathe. Breathe slowly, deeply and consciously. I need to remember to really look at what I see, and listen to what I hear. Attention is a key word. I take time every day to write, draw, record my dreams, and pray. Prayer has been described as talking to God. Stillness, quiet, is listening to God, the small voice within.

I have a hunch that in order for me to never have a bad day, I must be full of appreciation for the present. Instead of feeling regret over what isn't, I must be grateful for what is.

CHAPTER FOUR

If You Can ...
Sniff Out
What's New and Different

(Curiosity)

If You Can ...

Sniff Out What's New and Different

I loved living with Riley, observing his curiosity and desire to discover all that was new and unknown. His behavioral questions were always "What is this?" "How does it work?" and "Will it be fun?"

As basic as it seems, I feel that Riley's approach demonstrated a valuable way to recover, discover, and "sniff out" the magnificence in our lives. It may be a wonderful way to encourage the recognition of splendor in us all. I want everyone to recognize that "within," there is the ability to question our lives and then, put those questions into new and different life enhancing actions.

Since I lived in small towns most of my life, I have ordered many things by mail. The brown UPS truck was a familiar object to Riley. When the truck arrived, he would race to the door and wait for the delivery-man's steps on the front porch. It's not that he wanted whatever was being delivered. It was the opportunity to "sniff out" the unexpected, the new and different ... even the box. With great enthusiasm, he would use his paws, legs, mouth, and teeth to hold it down, tear it apart, and throw it around the room. The crunching sound of the tissue paper or the popping of the plastic bubble wrap was fascinating to Riley.

Nothing was too big, little or unusual (the box, a turtle, snail, fly, or roly-poly) for him to discover its hidden joys. All were fascinating playthings to Riley. It was as if they were carrying a red flag that said, "Guess what I am! Solve the mystery!"

I have observed that regardless of age or experience, life can be enriched by "sniffing out" the new. And in this age of "warp speed" technological advancements, there is always something new. One of the most exciting treasures I've unearthed in years is my personal computer - my own box full of hidden joys.

Several years ago, my husband's business, Martin Industries, was the first company to use computers in the area where we lived. Then, installing a computer meant there had to be special floors, walls and ceilings for vibrations, special air control for dust, even special aluminum jumpsuits worn by the operators. When I first saw their computer it reminded me of a small spaceship.

At that time, computers were so beyond my experience that I could not have imagined one being small enough to fit in my purse. I had no idea that someday I would own a desktop computer, a color printer, a portable iPad, and an iPhone. For someone born when television was also an infant, I find excitement (and pride) to be able to use a fax and a copy machine, a universal remote, and email. I can't wait to see what's next to try!

Beyond technology, discovery and curiosity have led me on many other diverse pursuits involving life … and death. It was not until my fiftieth birthday that I fully realized – someday I too would die. I guess 1'd always known I would, but until then it had seemed like such a long way off. I felt totally in the dark about the process of death. I began to read stories about the "after-life" and "out-of-body" experiences.

Facing the truth that we all have to die, it is inevitable and it's not a choice, I decided to discover as much as I could about dying. I'm sure it was no coincidence that about the same time a friend of mine invited me to study under the direction of Dame Cicely Mary Saunders, well known for her role in the birth of the hospice movement.

We traveled to a Hospice home in Plymouth, England, where we were assigned to dying patients. Our job was to be available to support and respond to their wishes. I shall never forget sitting with a thirty-nine year old mother of three, who was not expected to live more than twenty-four hours. Because of the excellent heroin pain control used in England (illegal in America), she was almost pain free, still mentally alert, and resting rather comfortably. As I approached her bed, I remember feeling so frightened and inadequate to be of any possible help to her. I took her hand, sat beside her and before I knew it, tears were rolling down my cheeks. She looked up with her soft, weak eyes, and asked, "Are you all right. What's wrong?"

I confessed how ashamed and embarrassed I was. How I did not have a clue of what I could possibly do for her. She responded with such compassion to my struggle. She said, "I know what I would like for you to do. Would you mind shaving my legs? They look awful. It has been months since they have been shaved and for some reason I want them clean shaven and neat when I die."

I was so relieved and thankful that she had asked me to do something I could manage. I grinned from ear to ear and ran to the nurse's station, asked for towels, a basin of warm water, body lotion, and a razor. I hurried back to her bed with the items and had the privilege of being of service to this brave young woman who wanted to die with a touch of what she perceived to be feminine dignity.

That experience didn't resolve all my questions concerning the mystery of death, but it sure was a powerful lesson on living in the moment without fear of the future or the unknown.

And as questions about death are such a natural part of life, so are questions about life. From an early age, one instinctive question for every human always seems to be "why?" The "why's" begin early, ask any mother of small children…Why do I have to go to bed, eat this, or wear that? Unfortunately, the longer I live the more I am embarrassed to ask "why," because I feel like I should already know the answer. Is it because I am too shy? Am I afraid of appearing stupid? Who knows? I do know that many young children give up their inborn desire to inquire when adults too often answer, "Because I said so."

At any age, asking questions are a critical part of continuing growth because resulting answers are an excellent source of positive life changes … for young and old. Never give up the privilege of learning. You've probably heard it said, "If you don't use it, you lose it." Well, regardless of what you've heard, it is possible to teach old dogs new tricks (Riley confirmed that). A friend's mother (eighty-seven years old) once said to me, "Darling, don't ever let your mind get sloppy." Current gerontology research indicates that the ability to learn does not decline until around the age of eighty-nine, and even then, it's only when one is trying to learn a new language or math principle.

My earliest, most passionate "WHY?" happened when I was only five years old. I was visiting my grandmother in West Point, Mississippi. On Sunday mornings, we would drive out in the country, over dusty dirt roads, to a wooden shack that had a pump organ and a few benches with tables pushed against the walls. On Saturday night, it was used as a honky-tonk, but on

Sundays she was there to teach white sharecroppers' children Bible stories. I will never forget my sense of "Why" as I looked at children dressed in clothes made of old feed sacks, with bare feet touching the rough wooden floors. There was a smell that was quite strange to me. It was not a dirty smell, but a peculiar aroma of coal oil and handmade soap.

We were the same age, the same color, the same gender, and yet so different. I had on a hand-smocked cotton dress and black patent Mary Jane shoes so shiny I could see my face in them. Even my underpants and slip were made out of soft white cotton batiste with lace edging. A barrette held a crisp taffeta bow in my shiny black hair. In contrast, they all looked skinny; their hair did not shine, but hung in strings like a Raggedy Ann doll. Their dresses looked as if someone had cut holes in those feed sacks, one for their head and two more for their arms. I remember feeling confused and uncomfortable. Did I make them feel badly by comparison? Why was it so?

Grandmother explained to me what their daddies did for a living, and to my five-year-old brain, this did not make sense. Their daddies' work was physically harder than my daddy's. Everyone in their family had to pick cotton, milk cows and chop weeds. On some deep intuitive level, I knew there was something dreadfully wrong with this scene. It wasn't fair. Why did I have what I had, and they seemed to have nothing? How could I make this right?

Today, I can still close my eyes and smell the poverty, and feel the pain I felt then over the unfairness of the situation with the sharecroppers' children. I don't know how a five-year-old child could feel that complexity, but I guess that's when I developed a heart for the "social underdogs."

I believe circumstances are the only things that separate

lifestyles and make us different. When I look at a street person, a bag lady, or a person standing in line for food stamps, I feel that same deep compassion and embarrassment I did when I was five and saw those children with barely enough clothes and food to survive. There, but for the Grace of God, go I.

I still find the exploration of the "why" perplexing. My life has been easier than others, at times eliciting self-imposed guilt and feelings that I should always try to pay God back. I will come home from a wonderful luxurious trip and feel compelled to bake a cake or casserole for someone in need, just to try and make up for the injustice of the system... another big "Why?"

Why do over two-thirds of the world's population not have enough food to eat, or decent work to earn a living? There are hundreds of reasons why. However, since I cannot fix every "why," I guess a better question for me is "what" should I do about it? Should I stop exploring? I don't think so; the rewards of discovery are too great. When I find inequities, despair or sadness on my life's journey, I now try to address them with compassion and understanding. Then I try to sort them. First, I sort those that I have the power and ability and desire to influence and then acknowledge and "separate" those situations that seem to be beyond my capability to resolve.

For the first category, I attempt to do what I can to alleviate the injustice. That is why I still bake cakes and casseroles. That is why I made a major decision to get a master's degree in social work, so I could work with battered women in shelters, teaching them that they don't deserve to be abused; they can become independent and value themselves. For those matters over which I have little or no influence, I remind myself that feelings of empathy and concern are proper, while guilt, depression or despair are self-destructive. For joy and happiness, we must never stop searching and "sniffing" out the good in ourselves and our lives.

Recently I came across a small, anonymous piece, informally and lightly written, but capturing the essence of Riley's message.

"I Am Tasting All That Is Possible."

I try to eat the food I need, and do the things I should.
But life's so short, my friend, I hate missing out on something good.

This year I realized how old I was. I haven't been this old before. So,
before I die, I've got to try those things that I did ignore.

I haven't smelled all the flowers yet. There are too many streams I haven't
fished. There's a treasure of discoveries that have never gotten on my list
of things for which I've wished.

There are too many golf courses I haven't played and I've not laughed at
all the jokes. I've missed a lot of sporting events, potato chips and cokes.

I want to wade again in water and feel ocean spray on my face.
I want to sit in a country church once more and thank God for His grace.

I want peanut butter every day spread on my morning toast.
I want un-timed long distance calls to the folks I love the most.

I haven't cried at all the movies yet, or walked in the morning rain.
I need to feel wind on my face. I want to be in love again.

So, if I choose to have dessert, instead of having dinner,
then should I die before night fall, I'd say I died a winner,

Because I missed out on nothing, I filled all my heart desired.
I had that final chocolate mousse, before my life expired."

"Anonymous"

CHAPTER FIVE

If You Can ...
Never Hold a Grudge

(Forgiveness)

If You Can …

Never Hold a Grudge

Recently, I saw a bumper sticker that read, "To err is human, to forgive is canine." I laughed when I first saw it. I think, because of the truth in those words, even Alexander Pope would forgive us for misquoting his famous phrase. Riley knew how to "forgive and forget." No matter how many times I left him, scolded or punished him, he was always ready to start anew. With his tail wagging and his eyes shining, there were no grudges. It was pure and simple forgiveness. Dogs are perfect examples of forgiving spirits.

Humans tend to react differently. At one time or another, almost everyone has experienced distress caused by someone else. These injuries frequently result in feelings of resentment, animosity or even revenge. Forgiveness is often overshadowed with knee-jerk reactions of "an eye for an eye, a tooth for a tooth," — if you hurt me, I'll hurt you.

But who really gets hurt if a grudge is held? Could it be the "grudge holder?" Nelson Mandela once said, "Resentment is like drinking poison and then hoping it will kill your enemies." Consider the words of well-respected staff members of the Mayo Clinic, "… wounds can leave you with lasting feelings of anger, bitterness or even vengeance … if you don't practice forgiveness, you might be the one who pays most dearly. By embracing forgiveness, you can also embrace peace, hope, gratitude and joy. Consider how forgiveness can lead you down the path of physical, emotional and spiritual well-being."

As children we act impulsively. Over time, we're trained to control our actions. We often deal with our emotions underground. I confess, I have struggled with forgiveness. I learned several ways of getting even. Maybe, I didn't speak to them or I talked about them behind their back or I was secretly glad when things didn't work out for them. I was always careful to keep these thoughts and feelings hidden. I'd be ashamed for anyone to know about them, but they were still there, in a corner of my mind, gathering mold and mildew. I tricked myself into believing that what you don't see does not hurt you. That's an illusion. Those unforgiving thoughts and feelings became the shadow side of my personality, the unconscious, the dark side of my soul.

Two examples come to mind, both involving "best friends." Sara Jane Smith was one of the first people I met when we moved to Huntsville, Alabama. Both being in our early twenties with newborn babies, we bonded very quickly. We talked on the phone, shared baby sitters, and supported each other in every way. Our friendship helped eliminate my fear of living in a new place. For several years the Smiths and the Martins did many things together, the husbands fished often and played golf every Saturday. We were the godparents of their children.

Gradually, some of Sara Jane's childhood friends began to migrate back to Huntsville to build their own nests with their young families. Naturally, Sara Jane resumed some of her old relationships. Feeling neglected, I became jealous, even angry. I started picking at her faults, at least in my thoughts. She was wishy-washy. She seemed to talk out of both sides of her mouth.

Sara Jane didn't have a clue as to what was going on in my head. She only knew that our relationship was growing prickly. I felt terrified that she would abandon me. I didn't want to be one of her close friends… I wanted to be her *only* and *dearest* friend. I was like a raging two-year-old whose mother had just brought home a new baby.

A similar situation occurred when we moved to Sheffield and I met my good friend Donna. As our friendship grew, she constantly (excessively) looked to me to help her make decisions and give advice. When I tired of her dependency, she found another friend to do the job instead. Once more, I was distressed. Even though I'd been the one to take a step back, I still wanted to be Number One.

Neither of these friends did anything wrong, and both of these relationships have since been healed. It wasn't easy, reconciliation took forgiveness.

Forgiveness is always difficult, whether it's others we're trying to forgive or ourselves. For me, I think it is easier to forgive others. I know I still feel some pain when I think of one missed opportunity to show compassion and consideration for someone in need. In the small town where I lived, there was an older woman who lived as a recluse. Most of the folks in town disparagingly referred to her as "the crazy lady." I had never met her but decided it would be a good idea to take her a basket of food and say, "Hello." She responded to my knocking on the door and said, "You can't come in here, I'll come outside. My family's ashamed of me and they don't want anyone to see how I live."

As I stood waiting outside her door, I was relieved and

glad to remain outside as I smelled a strong stench of urine from within. In a few minutes she joined me. Her waist length gray stringy hair was unkempt and oily. She had an old shawl thrown around her bony shoulders. I told her my name and she told me hers was Elsie. We sat on a crumbling bench as I began to tell her about the items I had brought for her --- a baked chicken, fresh grapes and peaches from our produce market and last, but not least, some Swiss chocolate. She showed no appreciation. To my total surprise she responded, "I don't want your food. I wake up every morning and ask my body what it wants to eat that day and then walk to town to buy it." She continued, "If you want to do something for me, you stay here and talk to me." Instead of seizing that opportunity to give, learn and share, I was annoyed. I glanced at my watch, made an excuse, took my unwanted basket and said, "I'll stop by another time," which I never did.

Shortly after that visit, I learned that Elsie was a lot more than just "the crazy lady." She was a graduate student of the Atlanta School of Art and had been a successful painter for many years before moving to our small town in the mountains. Elsie died before I ever made time to return to her shack. For several days and nights the winter temperature never rose above twelve degrees — it was believed that she froze to death.

Even though self-forgiveness is difficult, it is part of positive change and has allowed a way for me to see through my guilt to the hurt lying hidden in the corners of my mind. Releasing grudges (held against myself or others) cleans the slate and makes way for consideration, kindheartedness and harmony.

I have come a long way in learning to forgive since those

days with my two friends and my visit with Elsie. Much of my progress has been learned through the forgiving spirit of Riley. His basic approach to life helped me get on the right track. Whether forgiveness is "divine" or "canine," I certainly took a lesson or two from his forgiving nature.

CHAPTER SIX

If You Can ...
Dig to China

(Tenacity)

If You Can …
Dig to China

I have seen Riley dig "almost to China" to capture a chipmunk. Despite a success rate of zero, he was never discouraged. Each squirrel Riley saw caused as much excitement as the one before it. You would think he would have tired of continually trying, but each pounce he made was with the assurance of victory. Most of the time, the squirrel jumped to the trunk of a nearby tree, getting just high enough to taunt Riley with the possibility of victory. All the while, of course, the squirrel was making those little clicking noises that seem to say, "Nah-nah, nah-nah, nana! You can't catch me." Repeated failure to achieve his objective never seemed to dampen Riley's enthusiastic pursuit of the seemingly impossible. He was tenacious.

Tenacity is the foundation upon which success is built, and with time, Riley might have caught that squirrel. I believe it was Thomas Edison who said, "I haven't failed. I've found 10,000 ways that don't work."

I think one of the most determined things I ever attempted was to arrange to have the well-known author and activist, Gloria Steinem, come to our beach house on Anna Maria Island in Florida to conduct a weekend seminar on self-esteem for women. I had read her book, *Revolution from Within*, and decided that I could design a weekend workshop for women based on her book. At the same time, a voice in my head was saying, "Sure and you want to win the Publishing House Million Dollar Sweepstakes, too!" How could I accomplish this task, so seemingly impossible?

While walking on my treadmill, I was listening to Anthony Robbins' cassette tapes on Power. He taught about the power and necessity of developing a plan with a goal and a vision, and so that's exactly what I did. My vision was to present material that would help women empower themselves. My goal was to use Gloria Steinem and her book as a way to accomplish that vision.

With excitement (interwoven with more than a little doubt) I mapped out a plan. I would somehow arrange to meet her for lunch, present my idea and ask her for a commitment. "Sure," my inner voice said, "She's only sought after by thousands of people. Her book is number four on the best seller list and you don't have the slightest chance of meeting her." "One step at a time," I told myself. First, I will present my idea to her secretary (whose name I'd found by calling Ms. Steinem's office). Next, I asked a friend who knew Gloria, to tell her I would be calling her office about a great idea.

Then I tried to follow every affirmation practice and idea I had heard of:

I cut out a picture of two women having lunch together, and put a copy of her head on one of the women, and a copy of my head on the other. Every day, I looked at that picture.

I kept my "purpose" and my "goal" written on a card taped to my bathroom mirror.

I found a company that was interested in marketing the idea, if I could sign up Gloria.

I interviewed different women to determine what some of their self-esteem issues were.

I also put a date on the calendar ... reserved for lunch with Gloria.

It Worked! I felt like I had dug to China!

Gloria agreed to meet me for lunch at a private club in New York City. I was so scared I brought a rabbit's foot, a cross, and my grandmother's picture. I even asked for prayers from my women's group.

Gloria and I met at twelve o'clock, at the main entrance. The maître d' called me aside, "I'm very sorry, but I cannot seat your guest," he told me.

Shocked, I responded, "Why?" I could not believe my ears. This private club had just recently allowed women in — on the condition that they wear skirts. Gloria had on pants.

"Where do you suggest we eat?" I asked him.

"Well, there's a restaurant around the corner."

"No. ... where in this building?"

"All we have are private dining rooms," he said, "and you don't have a reservation for that."

"Well I do now."

In the elevator, on the way down to the private dining room, Gloria turned to me and said, "Oh, Nell, I'm so sorry. I knew better than to wear pants here. I just forgot." She was so gracious, and totally at ease.

Over the next two hours, Gloria and I sat in that private room and brainstormed the creation of an event for women. We decided to focus on self-esteem issues, because it seemed to be such a problem for women in our culture. We decided to limit the group to twenty-one people. Her requirements were that the youngest woman be eighteen , the oldest in her seventies, and they should be red, yellow, black and white.... she wanted a diverse group of women for whom this program would be useful.

Plans went smoothly and we arranged accommodations and reservations for the twenty participants. Together, Gloria and I flew to from New York to Sarasota for the seminar. During the flight, the stewardess came over to our seats and said, "Ms. Steinem, I would like to offer you a seat in first-class as our guest."

"Do you have room for my friend?" Gloria asked.

"No, we only have one extra seat."

"Then I'll stay where I am."

I was so impressed by her considerate response.

Several months later, after much work, personal situations arose that caused us to abort future plans for additional Self-Esteem Seminars. However, I shall never forget the lesson I learned about tenacity and determination. It still inspires me today.

All day long, I used to tell Riley he would never catch a chipmunk. Maybe he did, maybe he didn't, but he never stopped trying.

CHAPTER SEVEN

If You Can ...
Learn to Ask
For What You Want

(Confidence –Wants/Needs)

If You Can ...

Learn to Ask for What You Want

R iley, with no words at his disposal, was the absolute
best at being clear about what he wanted. He would
see a squirrel outside and run back and forth until I opened
the door. When he noticed me pick up the car keys, he leapt
up beside me asking to go. When I would slip on a sweater,
he would head for the front door. At the dining room table, he
sat quietly staring at every forkful, asking for a bite.

Sometimes Riley would come to where I was sitting and
lightly grab my arm with his teeth to show me what he
wanted. He would borrow a soft bedroom shoe or a neighbor
child's ball to fulfill his need to play. He had no concept of
not knowing his wishes. He simply let his wants be known so
his needs could be filled.

We are all created with certain basic physical survival
needs such as air, water, food, warmth, and shelter. We also
have intangible needs like a sense of psychological safety,
a purpose for living, and relationships in which we can
both give and receive love. All of these needs come with
the package of living and it behooves us to "Ask" if any are
missing in our lives. "Wants" may lack the necessity of life
sustaining needs, but they also play a major role in our lives
and provide a legitimate reason for "asking."

Unfortunately, too many children and adults fail to "Ask."
They have realized that asking for what they want involves

risk, the risk of a negative response. If it is believed that someone or some external situation is responsible for meeting needs, and a person receives a "No," then they are left with few choices. The word "NO" or the pain of refusal has too often extinguished the spark of inquiry and inquisitiveness.

To truly meet our needs, we should first learn to focus, to become clear within ourselves about what we really require and differentiate between our "needs" and our "wants." If our thoughts are not well defined, it is possible to confuse issues and pursue actions and directions that are unlikely to fulfill the "real" need or want. We may create a set of illusionary wants we think will gratify specific needs. For example, if we are seeking a feeling of self-worth, will "asking" for jewelry really make us feel important? If we are seeking self-love and confidence, will "asking" for a new dress really provide a lasting solution? If we are seeking companionship, will "asking" for a hot fudge sundae really take the edge off loneliness? Maybe, temporarily or superficially, but in reality, those "answers" are highly unlikely to deliver satisfaction — because the wrong question was asked.

I think sometimes our failure to ask the relevant question stems from fear. We need to be brave enough to reach out for the "wants" that will properly satisfy those needs. I say "brave" because it may be required to overcome the possibility of rejection or, as in my case, to overcome the cultural standards and expectancies of my upbringing.

During the time I was growing up in the South, many women, including myself, never held a job. We were never required to financially support ourselves. Instead, we were expected to become Southern housewives and, in those days, that meant we were supposed to be submissive to our husbands.

"I'd really like to have a new car."
"Sorry, Dear, but we're short on cash just now."
"I need to increase my household allowance."
"You have to wait a few months. We've spent a lot of money recently."

The car or the cash wasn't important. They were not what I needed. I needed a sense of self-reliance and of being a responsible adult. I was substituting unconnected wants to satisfy my needs. Because I was refused, I learned not to ask. This type of situation breeds a self-fulfilling cycle of disappointment and re-occurring failure. Many may not admit it, but "Because I said so," or "Because I know best," makes most of us furious. Some of us are passively aggressive, and like turtles, we pull inside. Others are like skunks, clearly aggressive, and everyone knows they are mad. The fact is, we want what we want and when denied our wants we become angry.

Fortunately, some of those discouraging experiences followed by objective self-evaluations have helped me understand that anger and frustration only breed discontent and are counterproductive to the full, viable and joyous life I seek.

We need to recognize that failure to get what we want from life may be because we have failed to identify what we really want and straightforwardly ask for it. *Failure to Ask precedes a failure to receive.* Through the process of asking, we initiate the process of receiving. Biblical scholars and laymen alike site the wisdom and truth of:

> **Ask, and you will receive.**
> **Search, and you will find.**
> **Knock, and the door will be opened for you.**

CHAPTER EIGHT

If You Can …
Learn From the
School of Hard Knocks

(Adversity)

If You Can …

Learn from the "School of Hard Knocks"

Early one warm and sunny day, Riley awakened us for his morning walk. The smell of spring was everywhere; it seemed like nothing could go wrong. Riley tugged against his leash, straining to get loose and to explore the territory. Since there was no traffic, we decided it would be safe to release him. Just as I unsnapped his leash, a car turned the comer. Neither Riley nor the driver of the car saw each other, and Riley ran straight for the front wheel. I covered my eyes, held my breath, and felt paralyzed.

There was a thud and then a yelp, as the driver slammed on his brakes. He jumped out of his car as Riley tucked his stubby tail between his legs and took off running. A series of frantic barks followed. At least he isn't squashed, I thought. Maybe he's not too badly hurt. My mind ran in circles.

Riley finally stopped, lying down on the ground, and let me approach him, but his large chocolate-brown eyes were still wide with pure terror. I knelt on the ground beside him and felt his trembling body, carefully feeling for broken bones. I talked quietly to him, relieved to find that his breathing was slowing down. "It's all right," I cooed. "You're going to be fine now." His tail began to wag ever so slightly as he gently licked my hand.

Amazingly, after a minute or two he got up, shook himself, and was apparently ready to go again. He didn't appear to be hurt at all. Evidently it had only been a glancing blow, so I hooked his leash to his collar once more and we proceeded with our walk, none the worse for the wear. I never really knew if Riley had learned a lesson or not, but at least that was the only time he ever had an encounter with a two-ton steel adversary.

As I reminisce, I wonder if I truly learn from those negative experiences in life which we call the "School of Hard Knocks" or as the British say, the "University of Life."

Sometimes, Yes … but more often, No.
"No, I don't eat Sugar Daddies anymore," after they pulled out two fillings.
"Yes, I still continue to eat popcorn," even though I've broken several teeth at the movies.
"No, I don't drink alcohol anymore."
"Yes, I continue to eat red meat and cheese," even though my cholesterol is too high!

Some people can be tapped on the shoulder, and learn their lesson. Not me. I have to be hit with a two-by-four. That happened recently. My husband Bill received a diagnosis of early onset dementia. This was not part of my plan! This just couldn't be true! I found it so difficult to accept. I experienced all the classical reactions: denial, anger, blame, depression and frustration. I suffered the "Why me?" and "Why Bill?" …but finally I arrived at the "Why Not Me!" Neither of us is immune to change or challenge.

With resolve, I'm now determined to do everything I can and not let "what I cannot do" interfere with a positive approach and an enthusiastic embrace of the future. I am realistic, but I will continue to use every affirmation practice

I know, whether it's cutting out pictures, making notes, or visualizing the best for the yet to come.

I am confident that life will continue to "tap," "knock" and "hit" us all, but thank goodness, I've had enough experience to know that I am not in control of people, places, or things. I once heard someone say, "If you want to hear God laugh real loud, just plan your next year."

Our lives are not unchanging; they are dynamic and constantly evolving into something new and different. That's the basis of creation. Many changes are expected and welcomed, others are not. When we are confronted with a "hard knock" or change that is distressing or difficult, I think we have simply reached a crossroad in our life's creation. Our future and our happiness are not conditional on those "hard knocks," but our lives are defined by how we interpret those situations and which crossroad we choose to follow. Life is constantly forcing all of us to make the same choice, which creative force shall we choose — the positive or the negative.

Even though the choice must be a clear-cut "either/or," it does not always seem easy for me. The simplest of issues can become complicated when clouded with emotion. That's when I try to remember Riley; he always kept it trouble-free and down-to-earth. He seemed to innately understand that life is good. If you can... recognize that life always offers us a positive option, it is our decision to accept or reject it.

When Things Go Wrong

"When things go wrong as they sometimes will;
When the road you're trudging seems all uphill;
When the funds are low, and the debts are high
And you want to smile, but have to sigh;
When care is pressing you down a bit-
Rest if you must, but do not quit.
Success is failure turned inside out;
The silver tint of the clouds of doubt;
And you can never tell how close you are
It may be near when it seems so far;
So stick to the fight when you're hardest hit-
It's when things go wrong that you must not quit."

~ Unknown

CHAPTER NINE

If You Can ...
Travel With
The Windows Down

(Freedom – Curiosity Enthusiasm)

If you can ...

Travel with the Windows Down

Life seemed to contain one exciting adventure after another for Riley. Each encounter with a new person was as enthusiastic as the last one. Each unfamiliar face seemed to be his "new best friend." Each trip in the car was full of so much wonder you would think it was his first ride. He would jump in the front seat as I rolled down the window, and out would go his head. Perched on hind legs, body leaning against the back of the seat for support, he began his adventure of freedom and joy. His ears became plastered back by the wind in his face. His nose twitched for smells. His eyes became glued to all that was passing. Riley was in utter Heaven.

I believe life can be an exciting "ride" for all if pursued with enthusiasm, curiosity, zeal and openness. It seems to me that we, like Riley, start life with those characteristics, but over time external influences sometimes have a way of tarnishing, obscuring or extinguishing them.

For example, having been raised in the South in a very traditional Southern family, I found that enthusiasm, curiosity, zeal and openness were accepted only if they were exercised within the strict confines of the stereotypical image of a "Southern Girl." I remember being told that I could not take typing lessons. The reason why I couldn't — I only needed to type if I planned to have a job and Southern Girls in my "social status" were not expected to work or financially support themselves. We were expected to be socially adept and be ready for an early marriage and children. As Southern housewives we were supposed to be compliant and submissive.

In other words, imposed environmental expectations functioned to smother my desires for freedom, self-determination and independence. But like many other G.R.I.T.S. (Girls Raised In The South), I have strived to overcome the constraints of that early training. There are numerous ways others have also experienced and surmounted obstacles to living life freely, enthusiastically expressing dreams and eagerly embracing the wonders each day. Traveling through life "with the windows down" inspires and us gives a chance to follow what we believe to be important and live with a strong sense of our values.

So *"y'all,"* feel the wind in your face and allow originality, creativity and self-reliance an opportunity to grow. If you do, I think you'll fully appreciate French writer Colette's comment —
"You will do foolish things, but do them with enthusiasm."

CHAPTER TEN

If You Can ...
Look for the
Good in Everyone

(Lack of prejudice –honoring each person)

If You Can ...

Look for the Good in Everyone

One of the amazing things about Riley was his ability to trust. Riley never expected to be hurt by another dog or a human being. Whether we took him on long trips or hauled him off to a groomer for the day, he was always quick to trust. He never met a stranger and he instinctively expected good in everyone.

We all start out at birth totally dependent. Infants naturally trust, as did Riley, everyone around them to meet their needs and to take care of them. As we grow, that inborn instinct to trust and expect good diminishes as we are taught not to trust. Over time, skepticism can overshadow positive expectations, depriving the discovery of the good that surrounds us.

Before moving to Manhattan, I had always lived in towns considered to be safe — where there was no need to lock car doors or houses. People were not out-to-get-you or do you harm. When I moved from our little town in Alabama to the "big city," I was stunned at how many people cautioned me against riding the subway or making eye contact with strangers and I was warned to "beware of the street people, because most of them are crazy or on drugs."

I'm not sure whether it was stubbornness or naivety, but I elected to ignore a lot of that advice. As the days and weeks slowly progressed, I began to say "Hi" to the people I passed in the neighborhood. One person was a street person that lived in a cardboard box close to the entrance of our apartment building. He was not young; he appeared to be about my age. His eyes were blue, he had a beautiful (rather dirty) Santa Claus beard and I could not detect any hint of an unwashed person. On one particularly lonely day, I decided to introduce myself. After all, I did pass him every day. I stopped and reached out my hand and said, "Hello, my name is Nell and we are neighbors."

A large rather soft hand took mine and responded, "Hello, my name is Albert."

That was the beginning of a delightful relationship.

Whenever I stepped out of our courtyard, rain or shine, sleet or snow, I looked for Albert. He would either be huddled under his old army blanket or sitting on a doorstep watching his world go by. He never asked me for a dime — he was not a beggar. He began to call me "Missy." I never passed by him without a smile and a blessing, "God bless you Missy." He was like an angel that appeared every day and assured me that I was okay.

On occasion, I enjoyed taking him food, sometimes leftovers or a few cookies and occasionally an American cheese sandwich. Whenever Albert disappeared from his cardboard home, I would be afraid the police had picked him up or he had gotten sick. But he always returned from his "wherever world" with a smile and twinkling blue eyes offering a sincere, "God bless you Missy."

As I settled into New York life, I also decided to volunteer in a soup kitchen that fed 700 people daily. As a server,

I had close contact with many of the "street people" as I poured their water or removed their plates. I overheard their conversations and witnessed for myself the "good" in the members of that widely disparaged community. Repeatedly, care, compassion and concern could be observed as someone would say something like, "Missed you yesterday on 42nd Street. I was afraid you were sick. You okay?" or "How's your mother? Is she back on her feet again?" Never once, during the year I worked there, was there an incident of violence or anger.

It is important to look for, recognize and look for the "Good," we should also envision it. An affirmative mind-set has the power to create outcomes that far exceed our expectations. Such a manifestation occurred for me one night when my sister and I attended a Broadway play. At the reservation window, I handed the man behind the counter my Visa card and picked up our tickets. We were led to our seats by the familiarly dressed usher in a black dress and starched white collar.

While glancing through the program waiting for the play to start, a man appeared at the end of our row. He was smartly dressed in a pinstripe suit and a Hermes tie. "Mrs. Martin?" he asked. Surprise registering on both our faces, I looked at my sister. Who was this strange man and how did he know my name?

"Yes," I said rather hesitantly, "I'm Mrs. Martin."

He smiled as he walked near. "I'm sorry to bother you," he said, "but I found your Visa card on the floor in the theater lobby."

"Oh, no! I exclaimed. I must have dropped it when I was trying to put it in my purse."

"Well, thankfully, it has been found," he said gallantly.

"How did you find me?" I asked.

"I asked at the ticket booth. They identified where you were sitting so I could return your card to you."

"Oh, thank you, thank you so much!" I replied in a stunned voice.

"I can't believe it," my sister whispered after the man bowed slightly, wished us a good night and stepped back into the crowd that was beginning to fill the aisles. A perfect stranger performing such a kind act — what an angel.

Repeatedly, I find that when you expect it and take an unprejudiced look, "good" can be found in the most unlikely places and people. I even experienced a loving gesture from a stranger in a freight elevator. It was in the garment district of Manhattan where I was working for a sweater designer as an errand girl. I was sent into the bowels of a warehouse to bring back sweaters to the showroom. After getting them, I started back up on the elevator alone in this seemingly deserted building. A couple of floors up, the elevator stopped and the huge metal doors rattled open. Five burly, smelly men got on, four white, one black. My throat constricted with alarm. Was I in the wrong place at the wrong time? I frantically searched for relief from the fear I was feeling and looked in the face of the black man. I saw love reflected in his eyes. I felt some sense of comfort as I sidled up close to him and slightly pressed my arm against his. When we finally reached the bottom floor, he quietly walked out beside me and said, "Come on, Missy. Let me walk you back to your office."

New York City is rarely known for such incidents of "stranger love," but another occurrence moved me deeply. On Staten Island I was teaching "Parent Effectiveness Training" to a group of parents who had enrolled because they were having trouble getting along with their teenagers. So for six Thursday nights, I returned to Manhattan alone on the Staten Island Ferry, arriving at the Wall Street terminal at 11:00 P.M. I had no idea how deserted Wall Street could be at that time of night. I felt dread as I walked through the almost empty cavern of the station to the poorly lit street outside. Where would the cabs be parked? Would there even be one? It was freezing, and the wind was howling down the tunnel between the towering buildings on either side of the street. I began to frantically look for the familiar Yellow Cab with a light on the top. In a few minutes, though it seemed like forever, one pulled up beside me. I gratefully flung myself in, quickly gave my address, and took a breath.

"Mighty late for you to be down here alone. Do you do this often?" the driver said.

"First time," I replied. "But I'll be doing it for the next five Thursday nights."

"Same time?" he asked.

"Yes"

"Want me to meet you each time?"

And he did, always right on time to drive me safely home,

and I knew grace was present. A lack of prejudice and acceptance of others often leads to spontaneous compassion and understanding.

Very memorable was the time I was in a grocery store in Sheffield, Alabama. A mother walked in carrying the most deformed child I had ever seen. I approached her as she was trying to push her cart and hold the child at the same time. "How old is he?" I asked. He looked to be about two to me. "May I hold him while you shop?" I asked. Tears filled her eyes as she placed his rigid, jerking body in my arms. Grace was there as we silently communicated. Our hearts embraced.

We are innately good, wonderfully equipped to guide ourselves in the right direction if we breathe, focus, and pay attention. There is a divine plan written by the Master Architect for each of our lives, yet we are still responsible for paying attention to the blueprint. God is the director of our script. He knows the beginning and the end, but we only get one line at a time.

We have all the right answers for ourselves inside, but sometimes we tend to be pulled off our flight pattern by people, places, and things (greed for material items, power, position, fame, and fortune). Care must be taken against such distractions or the loud signals of our spiritual control towers may be overlooked or forgotten.

My desire and goal is to be as good when I die as when I was born. It is taking a lot of gentle digging and awareness to find and attempt restoration of that "initial wonder" of who I was. The more I discover that wonder within myself, the more excited I am and the more easily I find that wonder and good around me.

Dr. Herb Barks, the former headmaster of a very fine prep school, is credited for coining the phrase that became the title of his book, "God Don't Make No Junk." Often quoted by theologians and bumper stickers alike, I can't think of any better way to say that "good" dwells within us all. To me, if I can discover the good in others, it seems to magically enhance my ability to recognize the good in myself... knowing that within us all is a spark of the Divine.

CHAPTER ELEVEN

If You Can ...
Live in the Now

(Balance)

If You Can ...
Live in the Now

R iley did not live in the past or in the future. He lived his life with balance, totally in the present. I'm sure that Riley was never concerned about "what has been" or "what will be." Just imagine — no concern about the future of meals, companionship, love (or squirrels) and no lingering concerns about the "what ifs" of times gone by. Riley always lived in the present moment.

It's a profound lesson, but I find that embracing and understanding this "live in the moment" experience requires a shift of thinking and demands considerable discipline. Unfortunately, like so many, I have lived far too much of my time in Yesterday and Tomorrow. Oh, what a waste of precious existence that has been. Our time here is finite and dynamic. *Time spent in the past or the future requires the forfeiture of the "now" and "now" is all that we really have.*

Of course, I recognize that memories and future dreams are an integral part of my life. However, I am learning that the creation of my reality is based entirely on my interpretation of the existing day, hour, minute or second. As the occurrences of our lives rapidly flash by, we instantaneously construe their meaning. If our interpretation is balanced, centered on the "now" and rooted in a confident affirmative belief, I am certain joy and fulfillment will be inevitable.

Recently, I read an online post about a young mother who was very ill with a terminal heart disease. For quite some time, she had been on a waiting list for a heart transplant. She had written a beautiful verse which I found very moving and captures the importance of living in the moment better than anything I can say. I am so pleased to share her wisdom and wish I knew her name, but unfortunately, she only signed her work as "Bluepepsi."

TODAY

Today I will delete from my diary two days: yesterday and tomorrow.

Yesterday was to learn, and tomorrow will be the consequence of what I can do today.

Today I will face life with the conviction that this day will not ever return.

Today is the last opportunity I have to live intensely; as no one can assure me that I will see tomorrow's sunrise.

Today I will be brave enough not to let any opportunity pass me by, my only objective is to succeed.

Today I will invest my most valuable resource: my time, in the most transcendental work: my life.

Today I will spend each minute passionately to make it a different and unique day in my life.

Today I will defy every obstacle that appears in my way, trusting I will succeed.

Today I will resist pessimism and will conquer the world with a smile, and a positive attitude of always expecting the best.

Today I will take the time to be happy and will leave my foot- prints and my presence in the hearts of others.

Today, I invite you to begin a new season where we can dream, that everything we undertake is possible and we fulfill it, with joy and dignity.

Bluepepsi
(author unknown)

Epilogue

Why Did I Want a Dog?

When I acquired Riley, friends and family wondered why I wanted the responsibility of a new dog at that time of my life. It was because one of my happiest memories was when I was nine years old and "Uncle Herb," one of Daddy's business partners, brought me a beautiful, red-haired cocker spaniel puppy. She was the color of an old penny, so I named her Penny – and she was all mine!

I let my two sisters and my mother and daddy play with her, but everyone knew that Penny was exclusively for me. It was one of the few times in my life that I remembered having anything that was just mine. She became a part of my heart that I have never forgotten. The day she had seven pups was perhaps my first glimpse of how wonderful it would be to become a grandmother.

I have had many dogs over the years. My husband Bill and I adopted one from the pound about three weeks after we were married. Her name was Boofie, and she was wonderful. Boofie belonged to both of us. She was not "just mine." And in the 48 years since then, we have had dachshunds, collies, retrievers, poodles, and a few other pound dogs. They were all remarkable, but none of them were "just mine."

Why did I, at the age of 62, want another dog? I think it was because that was a time in my life when I was really scared. We had just left Manhattan and were moving to Florida. I had spent seven years working and studying in the city and didn't want to leave. New York City had become my home! I was about to move to a funny island in Florida that I had only known as a visitor, a place where I had few friends and no specific work to do. The only people I knew there were my newly retired husband, my 91 year-old mother-in-law who lived close-by and visiting family. Life looked like one big question mark. Despite the warnings from others who told me I was crazy to get a dog, I knew I needed some kind of comfort. A dog seemed a perfectly acceptable solution to me.

The next logical question was why did I pick a Wheaten Terrier? The answer is simply because the looks of the breed appealed to me. I had encountered my first Wheaten Terrier in Highlands, North Carolina, at an antique store called Fletcher and Lee. Lee was the owner; Fletcher was his dog. Fletcher looked a lot like a F.A.O. Schwartz toy, with big brown eyes like dark pools of chocolate and a coat so soft it felt like an old angora sweater I'd worn as a child. I thought he was the cutest animal I had ever seen. He was small enough to fit in my lap or sleep in our bed, but large enough to not fear stepping on him.

Lee gave me the address and phone number of a breeder in Minnesota. I called her about two weeks before Christmas. Having convinced myself that a puppy was a Christmas gift for both Bill and me, I think I already knew deep down in my heart this puppy was really just for me.

When I first told Bill about "his" Christmas present, he was horrified. The last thing he wanted at that time was to be tied down with a new "responsibility." What a way to begin his retirement! But, since the puppy was treated as a present, it was hard for him to say no and in my typical "steel-magnolia way," I convinced him that it would all be fine. Preparing for the pup's arrival, I bought a crate, dog food, a bowl, and toys, saved lots of newspapers and found a dog sitter for when we traveled.

On December 22nd, we drove to pick up the new member of our family. I remember how nervous I was when we arrived at the airport. I was excited because once again I had a dog that was just mine. But, I was scared that all the things everyone had said about how foolish it might be and how much trouble he was going to create would come true.

When we got to the baggage claim, I couldn't have been happier. There in his crate was this wonderful new puppy! Fortunately, I had read a book about Wheaten Terriers beforehand and already had a mental picture how he would look. I was still shocked when I first saw him. He was almost black instead of the soft wheat blonde that I remembered of Fletcher. I had learned that these soft-haired dogs, like Lipizzan horses, are born black and turn their natural wheat color later. The only resemblance this pup had to Fletcher were his big, gorgeous brown eyes.

I had brought along a stuffed dog toy to entertain him and a soft towel so he could sit in my lap on the drive home. He was too exhausted from fear and the strange things happening around him to respond. He flopped in my lap as though he had decided he was powerless to do anything else.

We were like a new baby and mother. Riley was my constant companion. We walked on the beach and drove in the car to do errands. Other times he could usually be found resting in my lap. It was such fun to watch him explore and discover his new world. Some people say animals don't think or remember. I don't believe it. I think animals were created by God to share this planet and to help us learn how to live together creatively.

There is an old saying, when a student is ready to learn, the teacher will appear. Little did I know when I ordered this new puppy that he was a gift from God. Riley would teach me how to better live my new life of retirement in a strange and unfamiliar place.

The Swiss physician and author, Paul Tournier, once said that transitions are like trapezes. You must turn loose of one in order to grab another swinging towards you. The time spent in the space between trapezes is very scary. It remains true that transitions of any kind are always hard, oftentimes causing us to strike out in search of comfort. Life has a way of pushing us off our familiar trapeze by presenting us with circumstances beyond our control and current wisdom.

New beginnings are always hard — even when you're excited about them. I have found an amazing thing usually happens in those times. Life will supply you with a capacity to uncover abilities and strengths you did not know you had.

Hidden powers lying within us all, just waiting to be unearthed, will sometimes be dug up by something as simple as

... the tiny paws of a new puppy!

About the Author

Nell Martin is an author, motivational speaker, teacher and training facilitator. This book, *If you can ... Live like Riley*, has been years awaiting publication, remaining unfinished in a dresser drawer.

Nell has explained, "I'm so glad that I waited until now to complete this work. I wrote the first draft of this book when it occurred to me that the exuberant and playful behavior of Riley, my delightful canine companion, was demonstrating a framework for positive living. But as life's priorities kept sending me in many directions, my unfinished book slowly aged in the isolation of a drawer. It's thought-provoking — while I was maturing and growing, that initial manuscript remained the same. Now, I have been able to finish the book with a lifetime of experiences illustrating Riley's behavioral examples."

Nell Martin grew up in the "Deep South" where she graduated summa cum laude from the University of Northern Alabama and she has her Master's degree from Yeshiva University in New York City. Nell has developed programs and seminars for the Young President's Association and the Chief Executives' Organization among others. Some of her seminars include Self Esteem and Relationship Skills. She is a Certified Parent Effectiveness Training Instructor and has taught graduate courses for teachers through the Continuing Education Institute in Orlando, Florida

Currently, Nell resides in Sarasota, Florida, where she teaches, conducts seminars and speaks to a variety of groups. In addition, she is pioneering in the education and awareness of new paradigms in aging and elderhood.